War With MEXICO

by William Jay Jacobs

Spotlight on American History
The Millbrook Press • Brookfield, Connecticut

Library of Congress Cataloging-in-Publication Data
Jacobs, William Jay.
War with Mexico / by William Jay Jacobs.
p.   cm. — (Spotlight on American History)
Includes bibliographical references and index.
Summary: Discusses the issues, including the concept of manifest
destiny, that led to war between the United States and Mexico in
1846, the events of the war, and the impact of its outcome.
1. Mexican War, 1846–1848—Juvenile literature.   [1. Mexican War,
1846–1848.]   I. Title.   II. Series.
E404.J33   1993   973.6′2—dc20   92-46115   CIP   AC

Cover photograph courtesy of Archives Division, Texas State Library

Photographs courtesy of the Library of Congress: pp. 10, 12, 15,
20, 23, 29, 33, 42, 44; The Granger Collection: p. 13; Archives
Division, Texas State Library: p. 17; Bettmann Archive: pp. 26,
30, 53; West Point Museum, U.S. Military Academy, courtesy
Herb Orth, Life Magazine © Time Warner Inc.: pp. 35, 47;
Culver Pictures: p. 38; Chicago Historical Society: p. 49.
Maps by Frank Senyk

Published by The Millbrook Press
2 Old New Milford Road, Brookfield, Connecticut 06804

Contents

War With
Mexico

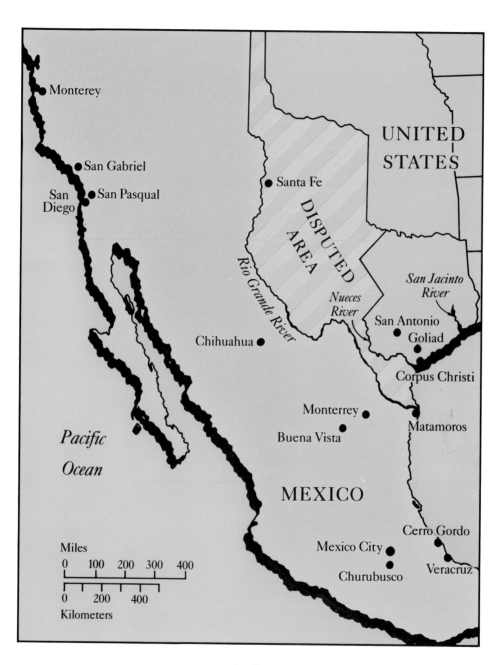

Monterey

San Gabriel

San Diego

San Pasqual

UNITED STATES

Santa Fe

DISPUTED AREA

Rio Grande River

Nueces River

San Jacinto River

San Antonio

Goliad

Chihuahua

Corpus Christi

Pacific Ocean

Monterrey

Buena Vista

Matamoros

MEXICO

Cerro Gordo

Mexico City

Churubusco

Veracruz

Miles

| 0 | 100 | 200 | 300 | 400 |

Kilometers

| 0 | 200 | 400 |

Introduction

THE AGE OF BOUNDLESSNESS

Shortly before dawn on a spring morning in 1846, American soldiers slept in their tents on the northern bank of the Rio Grande river, just across from Matamoros, Mexico. Suddenly they were awakened by what sounded like distant thunder. But rather than thunder, it was gunfire from Mexican cannons.

The American troops had been encamped on land in dispute between the United States and Mexico—land claimed by both countries.

A few days later, on May 11, President James K. Polk angrily demanded of the American Congress a declaration of war.

"Mexico has passed the boundary of the United States, has invaded our territory and," charged the president in an emotion-packed phrase, "shed American blood on American soil."

By an overwhelming majority, Congress voted to declare war. Almost overnight, thousands of men volunteered for military service, loudly repeating popular cries of "Ho for the Halls of Montezuma!" and "Mexico or Death!"

$\mathcal{B}$ITTER FIGHTING between the two nations continued until September 1847. At that time, American forces finally triumphed in a bloody struggle for control of Mexico City.

By the peace treaty signed in February 1848, the United States vastly increased its total land area. Territories in dispute during the war are included today in the states of Texas, California, Arizona, New Mexico, Colorado, Utah, Nevada, and Wyoming.

Victory over Mexico marked a high point in the American sense of a "boundless future"—a future without limits.

Such an idea had its roots deep in the nation's history. In 1815, at the Battle of New Orleans, General Andrew Jackson had defeated a powerful British army, marking the last time the British would fight their former American colonies.

In the years that followed, new states rapidly were added to the Union. Along the frontier, in the American West, new communities quickly sprang up in what had been a wilderness.

There was an explosion of technology, as one important invention followed another. Soon there appeared new railroads, the steamboat, and the high-speed printing press.

Meanwhile, ordinary people became convinced that the old limits to their personal advancement no longer held true. They could become rich. Nor did they have to show special courtesy to their aristocratic "betters." They could look to the future, and work for themselves.

Just as it seemed that the limits in *personal* advancement were breaking down, so too people began to believe that *national* achievement—that of the United States—was unlimited. According to some Americans, the territory, the boundaries, of the nation could be expanded indefinitely from the North Pole to the South Pole—and on the west to the coast of California and, from there, across the Pacific Ocean to China.

Some writers of the time felt that America eventually would have no boundaries at all, that the nation's proper limit was nothing less than the world.

*A*MERICA'S FUTURE was to prove very different. The Mexican War riveted attention on the bitter issue of slavery and its possible extension into new territories—Texas, California, and the Southwest. Shortly after the war began, Congressman David Wilmot of Pennsylvania introduced the Wilmot Proviso, proposing that slavery should never exist in any of the territories that might be taken from Mexico.

Although Wilmot's bill twice passed the House of Representatives, the United States Senate, with its many Southern members, angrily rejected it.

American troops eventually were destined to win great victories in Mexico. New territories would be added. But the question then had to arise: Should those new territories be open to slavery, or should they be "free"?

Hence the Mexican War, for all of its triumphs, would prove to be a turning point in American history, probably opening the way to the Civil War.

For that reason, as well as for its tremendous drama, it is a conflict that very much deserves our attention.

Stephen Austin established the American settlement in Texas.

1

"REMEMBER THE ALAMO!"

America's war with Mexico erupted in 1846, but the reasons for that conflict are linked closely to the story of Texas, beginning many years earlier.

In the early 1800s, Texas was a vast empty territory, a largely unsettled part of the Spanish-owned province of Mexico.

Then, in 1821, Mexico won its independence from Spain. Even before that happened, the Spanish had given permission for an American, Moses Austin, to bring settlers into Texas. After his death that year, the newly formed Mexican government, eager for new citizens, agreed to let his son, Stephen F. Austin, continue the settlement.

Young Austin promptly attracted some 300 American families, selling them land at far less than the $1.25 an acre then being charged in the United States. Those Americans who came had to promise to become Mexican citizens and to adopt the Roman Catholic religion. In exchange, they could buy thousands of acres of land very cheaply for farming and for raising cattle. By 1835 some 30,000 Americans lived in Texas.

Many of the Texans, including Austin, tried to be loyal, law-abiding Mexican citizens. But more and more of them grew unhappy with Mexican rule. In 1829 the Mexicans passed a law outlawing slavery, although many Texans declared that they needed slave labor to farm their vast landholdings. Soon afterward, the Mexican government ruled that no more immigrants from the United States could come to live in Texas.

The promise of cheap land drew thousands of Americans to Texas. This picture shows the town of Austin in 1840.

Mexican president Antonio López de Santa Anna
called himself the "Napoleon of the West."

In 1835 the Mexican president, Antonio López de Santa Anna, seized total power in his country, putting an end to local rule in the various provinces. He announced that he would crush any citizens who did not completely obey his orders. Those he had particularly in mind were the high-spirited Texans.

By that time, many American adventurers already had left the United States to seek their fortunes in Texas. Among them were such legendary figures as rifleman and explorer Davy Crockett, along with Jim Bowie, who often is credited with the invention of the famous Bowie knife. Most famous of all, perhaps, was Sam Houston, the former governor of Tennessee, who temporarily had lost himself in alcohol before settling in Texas to seek a second chance in life.

In 1836 the Texans declared their independence from Mexico and named Sam Houston as commander-in-chief of their army. As a free country Texas had a flag of its own with a single star. Thus it came to be known as the Lone Star Republic.

To crush the rebellion Santa Anna advanced with an army of about 6,000 men. On February 23, 1836, he surrounded commander William Barret Travis and some 200 Texans at the Alamo, a fortress in San Antonio. Included among the defenders were Davy Crockett and Jim Bowie.

Travis refused to surrender. For twelve days he and his men bravely held out against the attackers. Finally they began to run out of ammunition. Mexican cannons ripped great holes in the walls of the Alamo. Then Santa Anna's soldiers swarmed into the fortress. Still the Texans would not surrender. From room to room they retreated, but still fought on, with rifle butts, with knives—even with their fists.

The Mexicans took no prisoners. Every Texan soldier at the Alamo was killed.

Shortly afterward, some 400 American soldiers, surrounded by the Mexicans at Goliad, surrendered. Describing their prisoners as "pirates," the attackers killed every one of them.

The death of Davy Crockett is depicted in this engraving, published soon after the fall of the Alamo. Most accounts agree that Crockett died in the battle, but some claim that he and a few other Texans were executed later.

All across Texas and the United States rose cries for vengeance: "Remember the Alamo!" "Remember Goliad!" "Death to Santa Anna!"

Day after day Sam Houston retreated, with Santa Anna following him closely. The leaders of the Texas republic and many of his own officers pleaded with him to turn around and fight. But he refused, saying he was waiting for just the right moment. Meanwhile, he trained his recruits in the techniques of formal battle.

Somehow he also managed to attract another 300 soldiers, giving him a total of about 900.

Since Houston appeared only to run away, Santa Anna assumed he could easily trounce the Texans. They were, he reasoned, afraid to fight.

On the afternoon of April 21, 1836, Santa Anna's men were resting at their camp near the San Jacinto River. Many had fallen into their usual afternoon *siesta*, or nap. Their rifles lay neatly stacked on the ground. Suddenly Sam Houston and his angry Texans came bursting in upon them, shooting as they charged.

"Remember the Alamo!" "Remember Goliad!" shouted the Texans, thirsting for revenge.

In less than twenty minutes the battle was over. The Mexicans had been completely defeated. Almost all of them were either captured or killed.

In the dramatic triumph in the Battle of San Jacinto, only six Texans were killed and twenty-five wounded. Today, the city of Houston, Texas, stands close to the site where the battle was fought.

Santa Anna, attempting to escape in disguise, was taken prisoner. He promised to take his remaining troops out of Texas and to obtain Mexico's recognition of Texas's independence—but that recognition did not come.

Still, with victory in battle, Texas was free. As president of the new Republic of Texas, Sam Houston asked at once that his country become part of the United States. But Houston's personal friend President Andrew Jackson refused. He believed that one immediate result might be war with Mexico.

More important, Jackson knew that if Texas became a state it almost certainly would allow slavery. Antislavery Northerners bitterly attacked the possibility of admitting to the Union so large a

Santa Anna was taken prisoner after the Battle of San Jacinto. Here he is brought before Sam Houston, who received a leg wound in the battle.

slave territory. It could, they said, be divided into five or six separate slave states, each entitled to its own senators and congressmen. And those new votes would help to keep alive the ugly practice of slavery in the United States for many years to come.

In 1837, just before leaving office, President Jackson officially recognized the existence of the Republic of Texas as a nation. But, fearing disunity in America, he did not move to have that territory admitted to the Union.

The two major questions concerning Texas at the time—the issue of slavery and of a possible new war with Mexico—did not go away. Indeed they were destined to become far more serious.

2

MANIFEST DESTINY

For nearly ten years after winning independence from Mexico, the Texans had their own country. They had their own armed forces, their own president and legislative body, and their own debt—a debt that grew larger and larger each year.

Southern leaders in Congress continued to press for the admission of Texas to the Union as a state. But Northern antislavery forces refused to allow that to happen.

Meanwhile, to many Americans the idea of moving to the West became more real—and more necessary. The southern part of the old Louisiana Purchase territory, between the states of Louisiana and Missouri, was rapidly filling with settlers. As a result, many people began to look westward for new farmland.

More important, the Panic of 1837—one of America's most serious depressions—had produced devastating results. The price of farm products fell rapidly, making it hard for some farmers to keep up the payments on their land. At the same time, because of

ANTI-TEXAS MEETING

AT FANEUIL HALL!

Friends of Freedom!

A proposition has been made, and will soon come up for consideration in the United States Senate, to annex Texas to the Union. This territory has been wrested from Mexico by violence and fraud. Such is the character of the leaders in this enterprise that the country has been aptly termed "that valley of rascals." It is large enough to make *nine* or *ten* States as large as Massachusetts. It was, under Mexico, a free territory. The freebooters have made it a slave territory. The design is to annex it, with its load of infamy and oppression, to the Union. The immediate result may be a war with Mexico—the ultimate result *will be* some 18 or 20 more slaveholders in the Senate of the United States, a still larger number in the House of Representatives, and the balance of power in the hands of the South! And if, when in a minority in Congress, slaveholders browbeat the North, demand the passage of gag laws, trample on the Right of Petition, and threaten, in defiance of the General Government, to hang every man, caught at the South, who dares to speak against their "domestic institutions," what limits shall be set to their intolerant demands and high handed usurpations, when they are in the majority?

All opposed to this scheme, of whatever sect or party, are invited to attend the meeting at the Old Cradle of Liberty, to-morrow, (Thursday Jan. 25,)at 10 o'clock, A. M., at which time addresses are expected from several able speakers.

Bostonians! Friends of Freedom!! Let your voices be heard in loud remonstrance against this scheme, fraught with such ruin to yourselves and such infamy to your country.
January 24, 1838.

Opponents of slavery strongly opposed the annexation of Texas, fearing that the territory would be carved up into five or more slave states. This broadside advertises an anti-annexation rally held in Boston in 1838.

attempts in the 1830s to build new roads and canals, taxes were high in many Mississippi Valley states. When the depression arrived, large numbers of people simply could not pay their taxes. They had no choice but to move.

Finally, despite the depression, many Americans of the time were convinced that the United States was a very special country with a very special future. It was, they said, their mission—their "manifest destiny"—to spread the blessings of liberty and democracy to the less fortunate people of Canada, the Far West (California and Oregon), Mexico, and Central America.

As journalist John L. O'Sullivan put it, other nations, such as France and England, should not be allowed to stand in the way

> . . . *hampering our power, limiting our greatness, and checking the fulfillment of our* manifest destiny *to overspread the continent allotted by Providence for the free development of our yearly multiplying millions.* . . .

Great Britain in particular showed an interest in Texas, hoping to keep it free from American control. British manufacturers planned to buy Texas cotton, making their payments in manufactured goods. Other Englishmen hoped to convince Texans to free their slaves—something that probably would not happen if the territory became part of the United States.

To many Americans, both Northerners and Southerners, there seemed a real chance that Great Britain eventually would attempt to unite its territory in Oregon with California and Texas, thus gaining control of a vast curve of land stretching all across the western United States.

To halt such British interests President John Tyler began to work hard for Texas to become part of the United States. He had his secretary of state, A. P. Upshur, work out a treaty to do that. But before the treaty could be signed, Upshur was killed in the accidental explosion of a cannon he had been inspecting aboard an American warship.

Upshur's successor as secretary of state turned out to be John C. Calhoun of South Carolina—a leading champion of slavery. As a result, many anti-slavery senators took offense at Calhoun's vigorous support of the agreement admitting Texas to the Union. They feared that, as a state, Texas would become a strong supporter of the slave cause. Still other senators feared that if Texas joined the Union, Mexico almost certainly would react with military force.

In the election campaign of 1844, Henry Clay, the Whig party candidate for president, tried to avoid the issue of Texas, fearing that America would be split by it. But the Democratic candidate, James K. Polk, addressed the issue directly. According to Polk's friend former president Andrew Jackson, he could easily win the election if only he promised the American people "All of Oregon, all of Texas." Not surprisingly, Polk then declared that, if elected, he would work for the "Re-occupation of Oregon and the Re-annexation of Texas."

Jackson was right. Polk won the election.

Several months lay ahead, however, before Polk was to be officially sworn into office. Tyler feared that during that time Great Britain might be tempted to snatch Texas for itself. Some Texans openly encouraged such a belief, hoping to spur the American Congress to rapid action.

Tyler knew he never could win the two-thirds vote needed in the Senate to pass a treaty annexing Texas. Instead, on March 1,

By the mid-1840s, support for Texas statehood had grown. Here, supporters celebrate President Tyler's call for annexation in March 1845.

1845, three days before leaving office, he asked for that action by a "joint resolution" of both houses of Congress: the Senate and the House of Representatives.

The resolution passed the House by a vote of 120 to 98. It passed the Senate by a vote of only 27 to 25. Hardly an enthusiastic welcome for the people of Texas!

Still, on December 29, 1845, President Polk signed the document admitting Texas to the Union as the twenty-eighth state.

With that act, the die was cast for war between the United States and Mexico.

3

THE BRINK
OF WAR

Soon after Congress passed the joint resolution annexing Texas, the Mexican government broke off diplomatic relations with the United States. Mexico began to prepare seriously for war.

One problem, according to the Mexicans, was the claim of Texas to the Rio Grande as its southern border. As Mexican officials correctly pointed out, even when Texas was a province of Mexico the Nueces River—much farther to the north—had been the territory's border, not the Rio Grande.

Mexicans also feared that America would seize their province of California. As early as 1842 an American naval commander had taken over the port city of Monterey, thinking that war had broken out. Even after so embarrassing a mistake, the American consul had made Californians a promise: If ever they became independent from Mexico the United States gladly would admit them to the Union as a state.

James K. Polk ran for office in 1844 promising to serve just one term. He was the first U.S. president not to seek re-election.

President Polk first tried to gain his ends in the disputed territories without going to war. Speaking to Congress, he declared that Mexico frequently had failed to protect the lives and property of American citizens during serious struggles for power in that country. Nor had Mexico been willing to work toward a compromise treaty between the two countries.

Still, according to Polk, war might be avoided. He sent a representative, John Slidell, to Mexico City with specific proposals for peace. The United States, said Polk, would take over all past monetary claims (almost $2 million) of American citizens against Mexico if Mexico would agree to the Rio Grande as the legal boundary between the two nations. Secondly, the United States would be willing to pay $5 million for the territory of New Mexico. Finally, the United States would purchase California for $25 million.

Even before Slidell arrived in Mexico City, however, newspapers there spoke out defiantly against any compromise with the "vile Yankees." So angry were the Mexican people at the loss of Texas and the possibility of losing still more territory, that the government refused even to meet with Slidell.

With a peaceful compromise seeming unlikely, President Polk moved swiftly toward preparations for war. He ordered General Zachary Taylor, known as "Old Rough and Ready," to move his forces from just south of the Nueces River to the Rio Grande itself, close to the Mexican town of Matamoros. General Taylor went so far as to blockade the disputed river, stopping Mexican boats from using it.

At the time, President Polk still was experiencing difficulty convincing even his own cabinet members that the United States would be justified in declaring war against Mexico. How could he ask for war when his own nation was so uncertain, so divided?

Just then, word arrived from Zachary Taylor that on April 25, 1846, a Mexican force had crossed the Rio Grande and killed or wounded sixteen of his men.

No longer would the president have to ask for war against Mexico just because of past monetary claims by American citizens or because the Mexicans had refused to deal with Ambassador Slidell. Now, charged Polk in his message to Congress, "American blood has been shed upon American soil." A war had actually begun. "It exists," he said, "by the act of Mexico herself."

Responding with enthusiasm to the president, Congress said yes to hostilities: 174 to 14 in the House of Representatives, 40 to 2 in the Senate.

On May 13, 1846, James K. Polk formally signed a declaration of war against Mexico.

In the days and weeks that followed, however, opposition continued to grow. Months after fighting began, Senator Thomas Corwin of Ohio spoke bitingly against "the shame, the crime of an aggressive, unprovoked war." As Corwin put it, "If I were a Mexican I would greet you with bloody hands and welcome you to [your] graves." Greed for land that clearly was not ours, said Corwin, had caused the war.

And, in truth, Mexico probably had a stronger legal right to the disputed territory than did the United States of America.

Even after blood was shed in the waters of the Rio Grande, Polk still hoped to gain his ends without a long and costly war. One way, he thought, might be with the help of Mexican general Santa Anna, then in exile in Cuba with his teenaged bride.

Polk heard by rumor that if Santa Anna could return to power in Mexico he would agree to sell all the territories America wanted, including even the greatest prize of all—California. On orders from President Polk, Santa Anna was allowed to pass through the American naval blockade of the coastline.

Yet once in command in Mexico City, the Mexican leader broke his promise and took exactly the opposite course. In a series of stirring speeches he urged his countrymen to fight with all their strength and courage against the American invaders.

Americans were divided over the war—many in New England
opposed it, but support was strong in the South and West. This painting
shows residents of a small town reading news of the first battles.

THE SPOT RESOLUTION

Lincoln, in a picture thought to have been taken in 1846.

AMONG THE CONGRESSMEN who spoke out against the Mexican War was a tall, gangling, soft-spoken young man from Illinois named Abraham Lincoln. Lincoln took his seat in the House of Representatives in 1847, and he joined other Whigs in questioning the reasons for the war.

In January 1848, Lincoln presented Congress with a statement that became known as the Spot Resolution. In it, he demanded to know the exact *spot* where, according to President Polk, "American blood" had been shed on "American soil." Lincoln knew, as did Polk himself, that the fighting that started the war actually broke out not on "American soil" but on land in dispute between the United States and Mexico. According to Lincoln, Polk had involved America in an unnecessary and unjustified war.

Now, unable to gain his territorial goals with money, Polk was left with no way to win them but with force—with bloodshed.

Meanwhile, both sides seemed ready for war. Many Americans looked forward to expanding the nation's borders and were angry at what they spoke of as the "inferior" Mexicans for standing in the way. Mexicans, on the other hand, hoped to teach the "Yanqui" or "Gringo" Americans a lesson.

And the war came.

4

MONTERREY AND BUENA VISTA

General Zachary Taylor, leader of the American army, already had gained fame as an Indian fighter. Unlike his elegantly uniformed Mexican foe, Santa Anna, Taylor usually dressed in an old straw hat, a colorfully checked cotton jacket, and old pants. Still, his men respected him. They trusted him and had confidence in his knowledge of warfare.

Taylor's army, some 6,000 strong, marched 170 miles (274 kilometers) from Corpus Christi to the key Mexican fortress at Monterrey. There, behind high, thick walls, were gathered some 9,000 Mexican soldiers, armed with thirty-eight powerful cannons.

On September 21, 1846, Taylor launched his attack. His men were greeted by a storm of bullets and cannonballs from inside the fortress. Many Americans were killed, but Taylor's forces still pushed ahead, capturing two nearby hill positions. Finally they burst into the town itself.

*U.S. soldiers under General Zachary Taylor storm
the Bishop's Palace in Monterrey, Mexico.*

Mexican troops fired on them from windows and rooftops. The streets were barricaded. Fighting moved throughout the city from house to house.

Once, when an American artillery battery ran out of ammunition, a handsome young lieutenant, Ulysses S. Grant (or Sam, as he then was known), volunteered to have more shells delivered. Clinging to the side of his horse to avoid direct rifle fire from a line of Mexican soldiers, he survived, unharmed, to deliver his message.

Nearly 500 Americans were killed or wounded at Monterrey. But three days after the battle began, the Mexicans surrendered. General Taylor allowed them to leave the city, even permitting them to keep their small arms and six cannons. Impressed with their opponents' bravery, the Americans stood in silent tribute as the Mexican survivors marched past them into the countryside.

Zachary Taylor proceeded to win a series of minor victories against his Mexican foes. Then, finally, on February 22, 1847, at Buena Vista, he came face-to-face with General Santa Anna. By that time Taylor's army numbered only 5,000 men, while the Mexican leader commanded a powerful force of almost 20,000.

Santa Anna launched a first attack on the American forces but was beaten back. The next morning, he had priests burn incense and say prayers for his beautifully uniformed forces. Then, with bands playing the Mexican national anthem, he marched two full divisions of soldiers toward his American foes.

They were greeted with withering rifle and cannon fire from Taylor's forces.

Capt George Lincoln.

Gen John E. Wool

Gen Zachary Taylor

Lt Col Henry Clay Jr

Brevt Lt Col Charles May 2nd Drags

Sam Chamberlain, an Army private who fought at Buena Vista, painted these portraits of U.S. officers. General Zachary Taylor, center, is shown on his horse Old Whitey. Clockwise from upper left are Captain George Lincoln, a staff officer; General John E. Wool, Taylor's second in command; Lt. Col. Charles May; and Lt. Col. Henry Clay, Jr. Lincoln and Clay, the son of statesman Henry Clay, died in the battle.

Many Mexicans died. But still Santa Anna's forces advanced. Regiments from Illinois and Kentucky were forced to fall back. It was then that Colonel Jefferson Davis (in later years to serve as president of the Southern Confederacy in its rebellion against the Union) launched a powerful counterattack against one flank of the Mexican army.

All the time, General Taylor directed the fighting from the saddle of his horse, Old Whitey. Once, two bullets ripped through the sleeve of his jacket, but left him unharmed. Calmly he ordered that American cannons double the size of the ammunition they were firing.

Soon the bodies of the Mexican attackers began piling into heaps. Santa Anna had no choice. He ordered a retreat.

The Mexican army had been beaten.

By some estimates, Mexican losses numbered almost 3,500 in killed, wounded, and missing. American casualties were counted at half that figure or less.

When news of the American victory reached the United States, people on the streets at once began speaking of "Old Zach" Taylor as "the hero of Buena Vista." Most Americans—including President Polk—understood that, with such popularity, Taylor might well become the opposition Whig party's candidate for president in 1848.

Still, the war was far from won. And the pathway to complete triumph demanded not only the capture of Mexico City, but success in the Far West, particularly in California.

5

WESTWARD TO CALIFORNIA

The prize President Polk longed for most of all was that the nation would span the continent. With the addition of the Mexican province of California, America would extend "from sea to shining sea."

In June 1846, American settlers in the Sacramento Valley of northern California received word of the war with Mexico. At once they rose in revolt, displaying a banner of independence—the Bear Flag, with a grizzly bear facing a red star.

Spurring the Americans on was the dashing young Captain John C. Frémont—explorer, soldier, and destined in 1856 to be the Republican party's first candidate for president of the United States.

Frémont, commanding sixty men, did not just "happen" to be in the area when war was declared. His assignment from President Polk was that, in the event of war, he should work with the officers of American ships offshore and with the land populations in order to establish the "Republic of California."

*John C. Frémont raises the Bear Flag, proclaiming
the independent "Republic of California."*

Shortly after the fighting began Commodore John D. Sloat, cruising the coast of California, landed a force of soldiers and marines and captured the crucial port of Monterey. When Sloat became ill, Commodore Robert F. Stockton (after whom Stockton, California, later was named), took command of the expedition and continued the fighting.

Meanwhile, Colonel Stephen W. Kearny set out for California from Fort Leavenworth, Kansas, with his Army of the West. In August he captured the important market city of Santa Fe without a struggle. Then, with the famous scout Kit Carson as his guide, Kearny rapidly made his way westward.

At San Pasqual, California, Kearny was badly wounded in a cavalry charge by Mexican lancers. But, victorious anyway, he drove on toward San Diego, where he linked with the troops of Commodore Stockton. Together the two leaders defeated a powerful Mexican force in the Battle of San Gabriel.

With that victory, all of California was under American control.

While conflict was taking place in California, Colonel Alexander W. Doniphon had been left behind to conquer the province of New Mexico. On December 26, 1846, he captured the town of El Paso. From there, he crossed the Sacramento River to take the town of Chihuahua. Using cannons and cavalry to prepare the way for his infantry, he managed to win the Battle of the Sacramento at a total cost of one man killed and eight wounded. The Mexicans, on the other hand, suffered some 600 casualties.

*W*ITH VICTORY in the West a reality, President Polk could devote all of his attention to a campaign aimed at conquering Mexico City. A Democrat, Polk knew that his two leading generals, Zachary Taylor and Winfield Scott, were both Whigs—and that both eagerly hoped to become president of the United States.

Taylor, based on his dramatic victories in the war, already had become a national hero. Therefore Polk considered it a mistake to provide him a chance for still greater popularity.

Winfield Scott, on the other hand, had failed in a previous attempt to win the Whig nomination for president. Besides, he was over sixty years old. In contrast to the popular, informal "Old Rough and Ready" Zach Taylor, Scott was a careful dresser, a serious man who believed in strict military discipline. Many of his men liked to speak of him, in comparison to "Old Rough and Ready," as "Old Fuss and Feathers."

President Polk decided to appoint Winfield Scott as the general who would sail through the Gulf of Mexico with an armed force. He then was to capture the port city of Veracruz and go on from there to force the final surrender of the enemy in Mexico City.

If Polk's plan worked, Zachary Taylor would not emerge as the war's great hero. Such a result could be important since, after all, the presidential election of 1848 was fast approaching.

6

THE CONQUEST OF MEXICO CITY

As General Winfield Scott's troops landed on the shore at Veracruz they were greeted by massive cannon fire from a fortified castle overlooking the harbor. Slowly, carefully, Scott surrounded the castle with his own powerful cannons. Then, for three days and three nights, he pounded the Mexican fortress.

Finally, after much of Veracruz had been leveled by a flood of shells, the Mexicans raised the white flag of surrender. Veracruz had fallen.

Marching inland from the sea, Scott's army began making its way to higher and higher altitudes. Then, in the rugged hill country of Cerro Gordo, his forces found themselves face-to-face with Santa Anna himself. In bloody combat the Americans won. Following their victory they nearly captured the Mexican commander as he fled from his mountain fortress.

After the triumph at Cerro Gordo, American doctors joined with Mexican surgeons to treat the wounded of both sides. Before

U.S. troops land in Veracruz. Navy ships helped win the city by shelling its fortifications. They then blockaded the Gulf of Mexico, to keep supplies from the Mexican army.

long, word spread across Mexico that the Yankee invaders, rather than being the cruel torturers Santa Anna had described, actually were humane and caring.

President Polk, now sensing a dramatic victory for the two Whig generals, Scott and Taylor, dispatched a State Department representative, Nicholas P. Trist, to negotiate a peace treaty with Santa Anna.

Trist provided an advance payment of $10,000 to the Mexican president, assuring him that another $1 million would be sent when he accepted Polk's terms of peace. But Santa Anna, after accepting the $10,000, reported that he could not persuade the Mexican Congress to make peace. Meanwhile, he had pocketed the money for himself and used the time to build up his defenses.

Clearly, more American victories would be necessary to win the war, and that would take time. But meanwhile, Scott's standing as a war hero improved his chances for the upcoming presidential election. It was no accident that when he galloped by on horseback the military bands often played "Hail to the Chief"—a tune usually reserved for presidents.

SCOTT NOW MADE HIS WAY toward the enemy capital, Mexico City, some 7,000 feet (2,135 meters) above sea level and surrounded by deep and beautiful lakes.

Capturing fortress after fortress, the American troops pressed closer. At the heavily fortified town of Churubusco, Scott's forces came upon and defeated the San Patricio Battalion—a gang of 260 Americans, commanded by Sergeant John Riley, who had deserted the American army and joined the Mexican side.

Then, for two weeks after the Battle of Churubusco, both sides prepared themselves for the decisive battle of the war—the struggle for Mexico City itself.

The Mexican capital city was built on a high plateau surrounded by mountains. At its peak stood the massive castle of Chapultepec, a fortress that loomed as the ultimate goal of the American invaders. To conquer it, General Scott's force, numbering some 8,300 men, faced a Mexican army of almost 20,000 soldiers.

A romanticized view of the storming of Chapultepec Castle.
The soldiers did not fight in the full-dress uniforms shown,
and they had to use ladders to scale the fortress walls.

On September 13, 1847, the American forces attacked. They pounded the castle with blows from their artillery. Then, slowly, they began to make their way uphill in the face of blistering rifle and cannon fire from the Mexican defenders.

Ladders then were placed against the castle walls, many of them soon to be thrown back to the ground by the Mexicans. Still, wave after wave of American attackers forged ahead, bravely making their way over the battlements and then, at last, into combat below.

Inside the castle walls a group of Mexican military cadets called *Los Niños* (the children) struggled against the overwhelming power of the attacking American Marines. It was they who were the final defenders of the Mexican flag, soon to be replaced by a white flag of surrender and then by the red, white, and blue of the United States of America.

Today, in a monument at Chapultepec Castle, *Los Niños* are remembered as heroes.

As the American flag was raised above the castle wall, the last captive members of the San Patricio Battalion were hanged within sight of the rising banner. In the final seconds of their lives some of the men cheered loudly in honor of the very flag they had betrayed.

By the end of the day the American forces had swept across the rest of Mexico City. The city was theirs.

As the price of victory American casualties numbered 130 men killed, 703 wounded.

With the completion of military operations around the city in the next few days, the armed struggle for the conquest of Mexico was over.

THE SAN PATRICIO BATTALION

THE 260 AMERICANS of the San Patricio Battalion joined the Mexican side for various reasons. Some had experienced harsh disciplinary action, including severe beatings. Others had found their pay too low and joined the Mexicans after being promised land grants and money. Mexican leaders made a special appeal to new immigrants serving in the American army, particularly Catholics. Sergeant John Riley, the group's leader, had been sharply criticized by an officer before changing sides and joining the Mexican army before the actual beginning of the war.

Knowing that, if captured, they probably would be hanged for joining the enemy force, the San Patricios refused to surrender when U.S. forces attacked at Churubusco. Talented marksmen, they fought with bitter anger, but also with fear.

Eventually Riley and 74 of his companions were taken prisoner. Some were executed immediately; others later. Riley himself was first whipped and then branded on his forehead with a D—for "deserter." With fifes and drums playing, he was forced to leave the American camp. He last was seen trudging by himself into the wilderness.

Although the San Patricios were traitors to the Americans, they were heroes to the Mexicans. Today a statue stands in Mexico City in their honor. On it is a gamecock to symbolize their bravery and a pair of dice to praise their willingness to take a chance with their lives. The statue also features a skull and crossbones, to show the risk of death the Americans undertook for the sake of Mexico.

In this picture by Sam Chamberlain, members of the San Patricio battalion await hanging during fighting for Chapultepec Castle in September 1847. They were executed as the U.S. flag rose over the castle.

7

THE TREATY OF GUADALUPE HIDALGO

Although the war had ended, the peace had not yet begun. No peace treaty had been signed by the United States and Mexico.

Not wanting the Mexicans to know how eager he was for a treaty, President Polk ordered the diplomat Nicholas Trist to return to Washington. Trist, meanwhile, had begun hard bargaining with the new government that had taken over in Mexico after Santa Anna, seeing the impossibility of victory, had fled. It now was Trist's fear that, if he returned to Washington, the talks would break down.

Instead of leaving, as instructed, Trist wrote a sixty-five page letter to the president explaining why he had to continue the negotiations. Weeks passed. Then, on February 2, 1848, Trist signed a treaty at Guadalupe Hidalgo, formally ending the war.

According to the treaty, Mexico accepted the Rio Grande as its boundary with Texas. It agreed, too, that Texas, New Mexico, and California now belonged to the United States. In exchange, Trist agreed that the United States would pay $15 million to Mex-

*A victorious General Winfield Scott (on his bay horse, right)
leads his troops into the central plaza of Mexico City.*

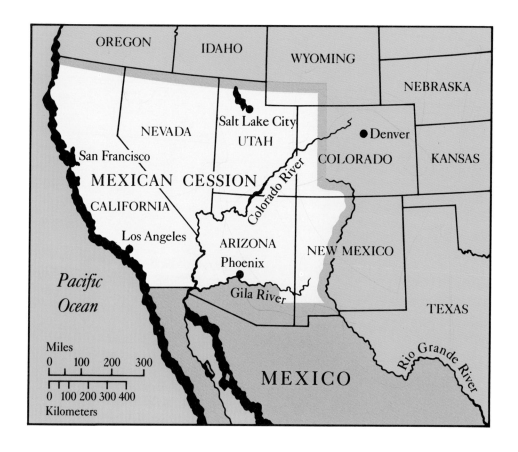

ico for its lost territories and take over $3.25 million in claims of American citizens against Mexico.

Polk remained angry at Trist for staying on in Mexico after officially being recalled. Still, eager for peace, he submitted the treaty to the Senate for acceptance.

On the one hand, he feared that antiwar Whigs would vote down requests for more money to support the American army south of the border.

On the other hand, Polk was concerned that many Americans might demand even more Mexican territory than was provided in the treaty. Indeed, some, both in the North and in the South, loudly were declaring that it was America's manifest destiny to take *all* of Mexico.

Nevertheless, most American moderates favored peace. And even the rabid proslavery senator from South Carolina, John C. Calhoun, feared the wrath of antislavery Northerners if the war was allowed to continue. Calhoun further believed that much of any new territory that still might be gained would be too dry to support the growing of cotton—the heart of a slave economy. He therefore favored Trist's more limited treaty.

When the Treaty of Guadalupe Hidalgo came to a vote in the Senate it passed, 38 to 14. Strangely, those who voted against it included both senators who wanted to seize *all* of Mexico and anti-slave Whigs who had hated the war and wanted *no* new territories at all.

*I*N NOVEMBER 1848, General Zachary Taylor, the hero of the Mexican War, was elected president of the United States.

A few months earlier, gold had been discovered at Sutter's Mill in California. By the time Taylor took office in 1849, Americans were mad with gold fever. Some of the gold seekers, or "forty-niners" as they were called, traveled across the plains in wagons. Many of them stopped on the way west in the newly acquired territory of New Mexico and simply decided to stay there.

Others boarded ships for the long ocean trip around the tip of South America. A few rich gold-seekers paid thousands of dollars to be taken across the narrow, disease-ridden Isthmus of Panama, a jungle shortcut where the Panama Canal later was built.

By 1850 so many Americans had arrived in California that it applied for admission to the Union as a state. So, too, did New Mexico. But if they actually were to be admitted, what would happen to the delicate balance of votes in the Senate between slave states and free states? Since both territories actually wished to prohibit slavery, tremendous anger mounted across the South.

Eventually the two sides agreed to a compromise, one known to history as the Compromise of 1850. By the time it occurred, President Zachary Taylor had died, and the agreement was signed by the new chief executive, Millard Fillmore.

According to the Compromise, California was admitted to the Union as a free state. New Mexico and neighboring Utah were to remain "territories," with their people to vote later on the question of slavery. Meanwhile, the *slave trade*—but not *slavery*—was forbidden in the District of Columbia, and stronger rules were made for the return of fugitive slaves, blacks who had run away from their masters.

At least for a time, from 1850 to 1861, the Compromise worked. Open conflict between North and South was avoided.

The seething anger, however, was only pushed below the surface. It eventually would explode into bloody warfare.

Meanwhile, because of gold fever, Americans eagerly moved westward to California, producing the very real need for railroad transportation to the Pacific coast. In May 1853, President Franklin Pierce dispatched James Gadsden, a railroad specialist, to Mexico to discuss the possible purchase of land south of the Gila River border between the two nations.

By that time, Santa Anna once again had become leader of the Mexican people and was eager for money. Before long, he and Gadsden agreed on a treaty, which is now known as the Gadsden Purchase.

FOR
CALIFORNIA
AND THE
GOLD REGION DIRECT!

The Magnificent, Fast Sailing and favorite packet Ship,

JOSEPHINE,
BURTHEN 400 TONS, CAPT.

Built in the most *superb* manner of Live Oak, White Oak and Locust, for a New York and Liverpool Packet; thoroughly Copper-fastened and Coppered. She is a very fast sailer, having crossed the Atlantic from Liverpool to New-York in 14 days, the shortest passage ever made by a *Sailing Ship*. Has superior accommodations for Passengers, can take Gentlemen with their Ladies and families. Will probably reach ☞ SAN FRANCISCO THIRTY DAYS ahead of any Ship sailing at the same time. Will sail about the

10th November Next.
For Freight or Passage apply to the subscriber,

RODNEY FRENCH,
New Bedford, October 15th. No. 103 North Water Street, Rodman's Wharf.

*In 1849, the discovery of gold in California sent
thousands of people rushing west. This poster offers
passage by sea, around the tip of Cape Horn.*

According to its terms, Mexico agreed to sell a huge triangle of territory across southern Arizona and New Mexico, but without an opening to the Gulf of California. Although unpopular with antislavery Northerners, the Gadsden Purchase soon was passed by the Senate at a cost to the United States of $10 million.

*I*N THE YEARS FROM 1845 to 1853 the United States of America had acquired Texas, Oregon, the territories won in the Mexican War, and the territories of the Gadsden Purchase. In all, America had become about one third larger than before. Moreover, it now was a two-ocean nation.

But the acquisition of new land was not an unmixed blessing. Those new lands were destined to create new problems, disputes that eventually would drench the nation in a sea of bloody sectional warfare known as the Civil War.

Epilogue

In the long history of warfare on planet Earth, America's war with Mexico does not loom large. In all, perhaps as many as 25,000 Mexican soldiers gave their lives. Some 1,700 Americans were killed in action, and another 11,000 died of disease. Yet the United States grew greatly in size as a result of the conflict.

At the same time, the battles of that war provided valuable military experience to leaders who would emerge as national figures in the Civil War period and afterward—for the Union, General (and later president) Ulysses S. Grant, George B. McClellan, and George Meade; for the Confederacy, Robert E. Lee, Thomas J. "Stonewall" Jackson, and Confederate president Jefferson Davis.

To this very day, Mexicans remember that the United States used the conflict to seize nearly half of their country. It was no accident, therefore, that during World War I America's German foes tried to tempt Mexico into fighting against its North American neighbors, promising that all of the lost territories would be returned to them.

Although some bad feelings still exist, presidents since Franklin Delano Roosevelt in the 1930s have made a special effort to encourage a "good neighbor policy." As recently as 1992, President George Bush proposed a broad North American Free Trade Agreement, including both Canada and Mexico.

Yet, from the standpoint of America's history, the Mexican War probably was most important because it stirred once again the bitter anger about slavery. Northern abolitionists charged that the South had brought on the war, hoping to add new territories where slaves could produce such crops as cotton. Southern leaders responded furiously, demanding that the new territories be kept open to them, as well as to the "peculiar institution" of slavery.

In 1861 the Civil War began. North and South clashed in bloody combat. As historian Thomas A. Bailey has observed, America's Civil War probably was greeted with quiet satisfaction by some Mexicans. They must have known that the struggle concerned, at least in part, whether those territories seized from Mexico would be "slave" or "free." Thus, in the eyes of people south of the border, America's Civil War might well have been thought of as "Santa Anna's revenge."

To some within the United States, the Mexican War was a high point. For, with it, the American flag at last flew in triumph from coast to coast. The war, therefore, could be seen as a preview of the future, of a time when the ideal of democracy would reign supreme around the entire globe.

But it was not to be. For in triumph there is sometimes tragedy. And so it was with America's victory in its war with Mexico.

Few could know it at the time, but for a while at least the nation's limits—in territory and in idealistic purpose—had been reached. The "Age of Boundlessness" was coming to a close.

Chronology

1835		Santa Anna becomes Mexican dictator
1836		Texas wins independence from Mexico
1844	November	James K. Polk elected president of the United States
1845	March 1	President John Tyler signs joint resolution of Congress offering Texas admission to the Union as a state
	March 4	Polk inaugurated
	March 31	Mexico breaks diplomatic relations with United States
	November	John Slidell's mission to Mexico begins
1846	January 13	General Zachary Taylor ordered to Rio Grande river
	March 21	Slidell rejected by Mexico and asked to return to United States

	April 25	Mexican troops attack American forces in disputed area
	May 11	President Polk asks Congress for declaration of war
	May 13	War declared
	July 4	Californians, with help of John C. Frémont, proclaim Bear Flag Republic
	September 24	Taylor triumphs at Monterrey
	December 12	Stephen W. Kearny reaches San Diego, California
1847	February 23	Taylor wins at Buena Vista
	April 15	Nicholas Trist appointed as U.S. representative in Mexico
	August 20	General Winfield Scott wins at Churubusco
	September 13	Chapultepec falls to American forces
	November 16	Nicholas Trist receives notice of recall from President Polk
1848	February 2	Treaty of Guadalupe Hidalgo signed, ending Mexican War
	June 12	American troops leave Mexico City
	November	Zachary Taylor elected president of the United States
1849		Massive Gold Rush to California
1850		Bitter sectional debate soothed by Compromise of 1850
1853		Gadsden Purchase of land from Mexico opens way for railroad route to Pacific
1861		Civil War begins

Further Reading

To help young readers learn more about the Mexican War, several books may prove especially helpful. Some of them are:

Downey, Fairfax. *Texas and the War with Mexico*. New York: American Heritage, 1961.

Fincher, Ernest Barksdale. *Mexico and the United States: Their Linked Destinies*. New York: Crowell, 1983.

Fisher, Leonard Everett. *The Alamo*. New York: Holiday House, 1987.

Perl, Lila. *Mexico: Crucible of the Americas*. New York: Morrow, 1978.

Reilly, Mary Jo. *Mexico*. New York: Marshall Cavendish, 1991.

Stein, R. Conrad. *Mexico*. Chicago: Childrens Press, 1984.

Bibliography

Bailey, Thomas A. *A Diplomatic History of the American People.* New York: Appleton-Century-Crofts, 1958.

Bauer, K. Jack. *The Mexican War, 1846–1848.* New York: Macmillan, 1974.

Bill, Alfred H. *Rehearsal for Conflict.* New York: Knopf, 1947.

Billington, Ray Allen. *Westward Expansion: A History of the American Frontier.* New York: Macmillan, 1982.

DeVoto, Bernard. *The Year of Decision, 1846.* Boston: Houghton Mifflin, 1943.

Downey, Fairfax. "The Tragic Story of the San Patricio Battalion," *American Heritage,* June 1955.

Eisenhower, John S. *So Far from God: The U.S. War with Mexico, 1846–1848.* New York: Random House, 1989.

Henry, Robert. *Story of the Mexican War.* New York: Ungar, 1961.

Johannsen, Robert W. *To the Halls of the Montezumas: The Mexican War in the American Imagination.* New York: Oxford University Press, 1985.

Merk, Frederick. *Manifest Destiny and Mission in American History.* New York: Knopf, 1963.

Reeves, J. S. *American Diplomacy Under Tyler and Polk.* Baltimore: Johns Hopkins University Press, 1907.

Rippy, J. F. *The United States and Mexico.* New York: F. S. Crofts, 1931.

Sellers, Charles. *James K. Polk, Jacksonian.* Princeton, N.J.: Princeton University Press, 1957.

Singletary, Otis. *The Mexican War.* Chicago: University of Chicago Press, 1960.

Stephenson, N. W. *Texas and the Mexican War.* New Haven, Conn.: Yale University Press, 1917.

Weems, John Edward. *To Conquer a Peace: The War Between the United States and Mexico.* Garden City, N.Y.: Doubleday, 1974.

Index

About the Author

William Jay Jacobs received his doctorate from Columbia University and has held fellowships in history at Rutgers, Harvard, Yale, and Princeton.

His international travels have taken him to the sites of battles in the Mexican War, such as Chapultepec, as well as to such fascinating countries as China, Burma, and India (the latter as a Fulbright Fellow); to the former Iron Curtain countries of the Soviet Union and Eastern Europe; and to Turkey, Morocco, Jordan, Israel, and Egypt.

Included among 28 previous books by Dr. Jacobs are a biography of Mother Teresa for The Millbrook Press and three American history textbooks now used widely in the nation's schools.